For My Teacher

From

_____

Teachers

Jokes, Quotes, and Anecdotes

**Andrews McMeel
Publishing, LLC**

Kansas City

09 10 11 12 WKT 10 9 8 7 6 5 4 3 2

ISBN-13: 978-0-7407-7238-2
ISBN-10: 0-7407-7238-4

Library of Congress Control Number: 2007934896

www.andrewsmcmeel.com

Attention: Schools and Businesses

Andrews McMeel books are available at quantity discounts
with bulk purchase for educational, business, or sales
promotional use. For information, please write to:
Special Sales Department, Andrews McMeel Publishing, LLC,
1130 Walnut Street, Kansas City, Missouri 64106.

Working with students is never as simple as yes or no, bad or good, true or false. Teaching is more like an open-ended essay exam.

Todd Whitaker

He who can reach a child's heart
can reach the world's heart.

Rudyard Kipling

I am indebted to my father for living,
but to my teacher for living well.

Alexander the Great

When asked for her occupation, a woman charged with a traffic violation said she was a schoolteacher. The judge rose from the bench. "Madam, I have waited years for a schoolteacher to appear before this court," he smiled with delight. "Now sit down at the table and write 'I will not pass through a red light' five hundred times."

It was my teacher's genius,
her quick sympathy, her loving tact,
which made the first years of my
education so beautiful.

Helen Keller

Thousands of candles can be lighted
from a single candle, and the life of
the candle will not be shortened.

Buddha

I'm a retired schoolteacher. . . . My favorite classroom story concerns a young third-grade girl who came to school one morning all excited. She explained that things were really different at their house now because her grandfather had come to live with them. Then, she said, "And he's sterile, you know!" The teacher thought for a moment and then replied, "You mean senile, don't you?" The child replied, "That too."

Daniel Kelly, *Warning! Cute Kid Stories Ahead!*

I have always been amazed by the high caliber of people who choose the teaching profession—a career without rank, riches, or fame.

Bob Chase

Education is the best provision for old age.

Aristotle

A teacher affects eternity.
He can never tell where his
influence stops.

Henry Adams

Every time my students get excited
about learning something new, I see
sparks shooting from their eyes.

Irasema Ortega-Crawford

One week I had four high school students mistakenly call me "Mom." Sometimes when they need help on a project, they call out "Mom" instead of "Miss." They are mortified when they call me Mom—everyone laughs, they get embarrassed, and I give them extra credit!

Cindy Maguire

There are days when you feel like
a blackboard full of wrong answers.
We just want to erase and start over.

Jim Dale

The aim of education should be to
teach the child to think, not what
to think.

John Dewey

TEACHER: (answering the telephone) "You say Billy Smith has a bad cold and can't come to school? Who is this speaking?

VOICE: (with assumed hoarseness) "This is my father."

Lewis and Faye Copeland

The task of the excellent teacher is to stimulate "apparently ordinary" people to unusual effort. The tough problem is not in identifying winners: it is in making winners out of ordinary people.

K. Patricia Cross

A new teacher, trying to make use of her psychology courses, started her class by saying, "Everyone who thinks you're stupid, stand up." After a few seconds, little Johnny stood up. The teacher said, "Do you think you're stupid, Johnny?" "No, Ma'am," he said, "but I hate to see you standing up there all by yourself."

Loyal Jones

In a completely rational
society, the best of us
would be teachers and
the rest of us would
have to settle for
something less.

Lee Iacocca

In the first place, God made idiots.
That was for practice. Then he made
school boards.

Mark Twain

Teachers are those who use themselves as bridges, over which they invite their students to cross; then having facilitated their crossing, joyfully collapse, encouraging them to create bridges of their own.

Nikos Kazantzakis

When I was teaching school in Brooklyn, one of my assignments was Hall Patrol. During one of my routine checks of the staircases, I found this big fifteen-year-old fondly squeezing the life out of an attractive young lady. I pulled him away angrily. "What on earth do you think you're doing?" Without even so much as a blush he came back with, "It's OK, Mr. Levenson, she lives on my block."

Sam Levenson

A teacher was asked to fill out a special questionnaire for the state. One question said, "Give two reasons for entering the teaching profession." The teacher wrote, "July and August."

Milton Berle

I can't give you a brain, but I can give you a degree.

The Wizard in *The Wizard of Oz*

My hunch is that anyone who has ever been able to sustain good work has had at least one person—and often many—who have believed in him or her. We just don't get to be competent human beings without a lot of different investments from others.

Fred Rogers

Children are uncut jewels with invaluable potential. Teachers are jewelers with tools for making futures priceless.

Angela Harper Brooks

Good teachers are costly, but bad teachers cost more.

Bob Talbert

TEACHER: "Tommy, where was the Declaration of Independence signed?"

TOMMY: "At the bottom, I guess."

The dream begins with a teacher
who believes in you, who tugs and
pushes and leads you to the next
plateau, sometimes poking you with
a sharp stick called "truth."

Dan Rather

A teacher's constant task is to take
a roomful of live wires and see to it
that they're grounded.

E. C. McKenzie

Teachers are expected to reach unattainable goals with inadequate tools. The miracle is that most times they accomplish this impossible task.

Haim Ginott

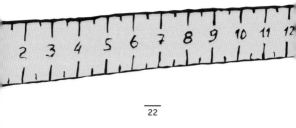

A mountaineer took his son to a school to enroll him. "My boy's after larnin', what d'ya have?" he asked the teacher. "We offer English, trigonometry, spelling, etc.," she replied. "Well, give him some of that thar trigernometry; he's the worst shot in the family."

Lewis and Faye Copeland

Even one caring adult in the life of a young person can make all the difference in the world.

Hillary Rodham Clinton

We learn by teaching.

James Howell

The difference between good teachers and great teachers is that great teachers have mastered the art of teaching people things they didn't know they needed to learn.

Jeff Wahl

If you can read this, thank a teacher.

Anonymous

There is an old saying that the course of civilization is a race between catastrophe and education. In a democracy such as ours, we must make sure that education wins the race.

John F. Kennedy

I like a teacher who gives you something to take home to think about besides homework.

Lily Tomlin as "Edith Ann"

FIRST STUDENT: "How old is Professor Green?"
SECOND STUDENT: "Pretty old. They say he used to teach Shakespeare."

Mildred Meiers and Jack Knapp

The career you have selected is one of the most difficult jobs you'll ever do, but educating children is also the noblest profession, and there aren't many who can handle the workload with dignity and compassion.

Lynn Marie Rominger et al.

Teaching is the art of sharing.

Abraham Joshua Heschel

Teachers, no matter what grade level or subject they teach, know that nothing is more crucial (or rewarding) than helping a student become a better reader.

Sandra Feldman

Education: the path from cocky
ignorance to miserable uncertainity.

Mark Twain

The excitement of learning
separates youth from old age. As
long as you're learning, you're
not old.

Rosalyn S. Yalow

They may forget what you said, but they will never forget how you made them feel.

Carl W. Buechner

Many teachers say they enter the profession in part because it is a form of public service—a way of making a contribution to society.

David Haselkorn

True terror is to wake up one morning and discover that your high school class is running the country.

Kurt Vonnegut Jr.

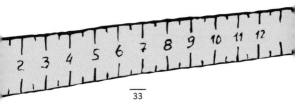

If a doctor, lawyer, or dentist had forty people in his office at one time, all of whom had different needs, and some of whom didn't want to be there and were causing trouble, and the doctor, lawyer, or dentist, without assistance, had to treat them all with professional excellence for nine months, then he might have some conception of the classroom teacher's job.

Donald D. Quinn

A good teacher must be able to put himself in the place of those who find learning hard.

Eliphas Levi

Teachers are, without question, the heartbeat of a successful school.

Ernest Boyer

A Minneapolis, Minnesota, high school teacher hung this sign under the clock in her classroom: "Time will pass . . . will you?"

James E. Myers

It is not the brains that matter most, but that which guides them—the character, the heart, generous qualities, progressive ideas.

Fyodor Dostoyevsky

Smartness runs in my family. When I went to school I was so smart my teacher was in my class for five years.

George Burns

Mothers are great. When I was teaching, a mother once wrote me a note about her son. It said, "If Gregory is a bad boy, don't slap him, slap the boy next to him. Gregory will get the idea."

Sam Levenson

Teaching is about both the students and teacher learning together, and that's when miracles occur.

Jackie Waldman

In teaching you cannot see the fruit of a day's work. It is invisible and remains so, maybe for twenty years.

Jacques Barzun

In knowing who you are and being willing to share your honest self with the children in your life, you're participating in "child care."

Fred Rogers

A smile from your teacher is like an unofficial A.

Jim Dale

She used to be a teacher but she has
no class now.

Fred Allen

Give the pupils something to do, not
something to learn; and the doing
is of such a nature as to demand
thinking; learning naturally results.

John Dewey

TEACHER: "This is the fourth time you've been so bad that I've had to punish you this week. What do you care to say about your actions?"

STUDENT: "Thank God it's Friday!"

James E. Myers

Too often we underestimate the power of a touch, a smile, a kind word, a listening ear, an honest compliment, or the smallest act of caring, all of which have the potential to turn a life around.

Leo Buscaglia

Education is our passport to the future, for tomorrow belongs to the people who prepare for it today.

Malcolm X

The greatest sign of success for a teacher . . . is to be able to say, "The children are now working as if I did not exist."

Maria Montessori

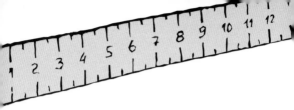

"What is the plural of man, Willie?"
 asked the teacher.
"Men," answered Willie.
"And, the plural of child?"
"Twins," was the unexpected reply.

Lewis and Faye Copeland

Sometimes a person's mind is stretched by a new idea and never does go back to its old dimensions.

Oliver Wendell Holmes

May 3 is National Teacher Day, a time for honoring teachers and recognizing the lasting contributions they make to our lives.

"And how do you like going to school, Roger?" a kindly lady inquired of a very small lad.

"Oh, I like going all right," the boy replied, "and I like coming back too. It's having to stay after I get there that bothers me."

Jacob M. Braude

When I longed to see the world,
A teacher gave me wings . . .
And urged me always to explore
The in and out of things.

Patrick Regan

The mind is not a vessel to be filled
but a fire to be kindled.

Plutarch

Discipline is not the enemy
of enthusiasm.

Principal Joe Clark in *Lean on Me*

Teaching, after all, is about *knowing*
children well.

Vito Perrone

One day in school, the teacher wrote on the blackboard: "I ain't had no fun at all last week." She turned to her class and said, "Now, what should I do to correct that?" A shy student stood up and replied meekly, "Maybe you should get a boyfriend."

Helen Rudin

The mediocre teacher tells. The good teacher explains. The superior teacher demonstrates. The great teacher inspires.

William A. Ward

The test of a good teacher is not how many questions he can ask his pupils that they will answer readily, but how many questions he inspires them to ask him which he finds it hard to answer.

Alice Wellington Rollins

BILLY: "I got a hundred in school today."

MOTHER: "That's wonderful, Billy. What did you get a hundred in?"

BILLY: "Two things. I got fifty in spelling and fifty in arithmetic."

Joseph Rosenbloom

Teaching kids to count is fine, but teaching them what counts is best.

Bob Talbert

An understanding heart is everything in a teacher, and cannot be esteemed highly enough.

Carl Jung

Nothing quite compares to a student's face lighting up to learning.

Kathleen Feeney Jonson

When one teacher told his class to write the longest sentence they could compose, a bright spark wrote: "Imprisonment for life"!

Michael Kilgarriff

Anyone who stops learning is old, whether at twenty or eighty. Anyone who keeps learning stays young.

Henry Ford

Knowledge is love and light and vision.

Helen Keller

That energy which makes a child
hard to manage is the energy,
which afterward makes him a
manager of life.

James Baldwin

The classroom and teacher occupy the most important part, the most important position of the human fabric. . . . In the schoolhouse we have the heart of the whole society.

Henry Golden

Kids' views are often just as valid as the teachers'. The best teachers are the ones that know that.

Morley Safer

Every day that we spend without learning something is a day lost.

Ludwig van Beethoven

There's no word in the language that I revere more than "teacher." None. My heart sings when a kid refers to me as his teacher, and it always has. I've honored myself and the entire family of man by becoming a teacher.

Pat Conroy, *The Prince of Tides*

Teaching is not a profession for the weak or the lazy. It is hard work and carries a huge responsibility. For the true professional, however, teaching brings rewards not found in any other field.

Patricia Woodward

Appreciation is that happy day in the life of a teacher when a student says, "I enjoyed being in your class today."

Paul McClure

Pace yourself. You have to stay ahead of the fastest student and remain right alongside the slowest pupil at the same time.

Robert D. Ramsey

One teacher recently retired with a half-million dollars after thirty years of working hard, caring, dedicating herself, and totally immersing herself in the problems of the students. That gave her $50. The rest came from the death of a rich uncle.

Milton Berle

I touch the future. I teach.

Christa McAuliffe

A mind is a terrible thing to waste.

United Negro College Fund slogan

A teacher's major contribution may pop out anonymously in the life of some ex-student's grandchild.

Wendell Berry

The secret in education lies in respecting the student.

Ralph Waldo Emerson

Teaching is not only what I do, but who I am.

Juley Harper

The important thing is not so much that every child should be taught, as that every child should be given the wish to learn.

John Lubbock

If I accept you as you are, I will make you worse; however, if I treat you as though you are what you are capable of becoming, I help you become that.

Johann Wolfgang von Goethe

The thing I remember best about successful people I've met all through the years is their obvious delight in what they're doing . . . and it seems to have very little to do with worldly success. They just love what they're doing, and they love it in front of others.

Fred Rogers

Little Billy brought home his report card. His mother took him to task for all the low grades. Little Billy responded, "It's got its good side too. You know darn well I'm not cheating!"

Milton Berle

The teacher is one who makes
two ideas grow where only
one grew before.

Elbert Hubbard

Teaching is the greatest
act of optimism.

Colleen Wilcox

Better than a thousand days of
diligent study is one day with
a great teacher.

Japanese proverb

In a hundred years from now it will not matter what my bank account was, the type of house I lived in, or the kinds of clothes I wore, but the world may be much different because I was important in the life of a child.

Anonymous

REASONS TO BE A TEACHER

- You want to get home before the rush hour starts, even if you have to drive a 1968 Dodge Dart to do it.
- You want your summers free so you can scrape together a living by driving a cab, tending bar, and selling Fuller brushes.

Art Peterson

Unfortunately, the popular English teacher came down with the flu and had to be hospitalized. There, she received countless get-well cards addressed to the ill literate.

Jeff Rovin

The best teacher is the one
who suggests rather than
dogmatizes, and inspires his listener
with the wish to teach himself.

Edward Robert Bulwer-Lytton

The teacher who is indeed wise does not bid you to enter the house of his wisdom but rather leads you to the threshold of your mind.

Kahlil Gibran

One of the many things I envy about teachers is the joy they feel when students come back to tell them how grateful they are for what they were taught.

Jay Mathews

Teacher's True Story

Our routine for show-and-tell involves standing in a circle and each child hiding their special item behind their back until it is their time to share. As I announced Emily's turn, Benjamin shouted out, "I know what she has! She has diarrhea!" Not knowing for sure, I was a little relieved when she pulled out her diary.

Amy Brown

Teachers provide a social and intellectual environment in which students can learn.

James MacGregor Burns

Over the years I've found that it is only by listening to others that you can leave yourself open to learning.

Julia Child

Every child needs a champion.

Hillary Rodham Clinton

TEACHER: "Sarah, what was the first thing James I did on coming to the throne?"
SARAH: "He sat down, miss."

Michael Kilgarriff

Children are like wet cement. Whatever falls on them makes an impression.

Haim Ginott

Good teaching is more a giving of
right questions than a giving
of right answers.

Josef Albers

Teachers, I believe, are the most
responsible and important members
of society because their professional
efforts affect the fate of the earth.

Helen Caldicott

It must be tremendously interesting to be a schoolmaster, to watch boys grow up and help them along; to see their characters develop and what they become when they leave school and the world gets hold of them. I don't see how you could ever get old in a world that's always young.

Katherine in *Goodbye, Mr. Chips*

The goal of education is to replace an empty mind with an open mind.

Malcolm Forbes

Teacher's True Story

Little Tori gave me a great big
hug when she came to class one
morning. I noticed that she smelled
real nice and told her so.
She replied, "Thanks! I put on some
of my dad's boyfume."

Amy Brown

If I were in charge of the universe, good teachers would earn far more than cabinet ministers; the latter are replaceable, the former are not.

Phyllis Theroux

There are three requisites for good teaching: One, you have to love your subject; two, you have to know what you're talking about; three, you have to like students. The question is whether you can make an impact on somebody's mind and soul.

Pierce Lewis

TEACHER: "Barbara, finish off this proverb: one good turn . . ."
BARBARA: "One good turn gives you all the blankets!"

Michael Kilgarriff

I know, for me, that teaching is about making surprises and moments for kids that they will never forget.

Ron Clark

When I give a lecture, I accept that people look at their watches, but what I do not tolerate is when they look at it and raise it to their ear to find out if it stopped.

Marcel Achard

All across our country, there are good people insisting on a good start for the young, and doing something about it.

Fred Rogers

We cannot always build the future for our youth, but we can build our youth for the future.

Franklin D. Roosevelt

Teaching is the essential profession—the one that makes all other professions possible.

David Haselkorn

A teacher asked the class to name the states of the United States. One child responded so promptly and accurately as to bring forth this comment from the teacher: "You did very well—much better than I could have done at your age." "Yes, you could," said the child consolingly, "there were only thirteen then."

Lewis and Faye Copeland

What a wonderful world teachers work and live in! Every year we get a fresh start, a new beginning, and another chance to touch a life and enrich our own.

Patricia Woodward

The aspiring psychiatrists were attending their first class on emotional extremes.

"Just to establish some parameters," said the professor, "Mr. Nichols: What is the opposite of joy?"

"Sadness," said the student.

"And the opposite of depression, Ms. Biggs?"

"Elation."

"How about the opposite of woe, Mr. Wilson?"

"I believe that's giddyap," the student replied.

Jeff Rovin

Teachers can change lives with
just the right mix of chalk
and challenges.

Joyce A. Myers

A schoolteacher who had been telling a class of small pupils the story of the discovery of America by Columbus ended with: "And all this happened more than four hundred years ago." A little boy, his eyes wide open with wonder, said, after a moment's thought: "Gee! What a memory you've got."

Lewis and Faye Copeland

To waken interest and kindle enthusiasm is the sure way to teach easily and successfully.

Tryon Edwards

Life is not a holiday, but an education.

John Ed Patten

It is one of the great pleasures of a
student's life to buy a heap of books
at the beginning of the autumn.
Here, he fancies, are all the secrets.

Robert Lynd

If he ever lives to be an adult, it'll be
a testament to his teachers' patience
and his parents' self-control!

Milton Berle

Without education, you're not going anywhere in this world.

Malcolm X

Where there is an open mind, there will always be a frontier.

Charles F. Kettering

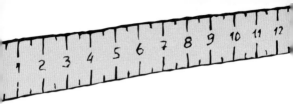

Teachers are ordinary people
who are asked to perform an
extraordinary job, and most do so
with persistence and optimism but
often with too little understanding
from others.

Catherine Collins and Douglas Frantz

The task of the modern educator
is not to cut down jungles, but to
irrigate deserts.

C. S. Lewis

Crazy Things Kids Write on Tests

- The future of "I give" is "I take."
- To prevent head colds, use an agonizer to spray into the nose until it drips into the throat.
- Heredity means that . . . if your grandpa didn't have any children, then your daddy probably wouldn't have had any, and neither would you, probably.
- The climate is hottest next to the Creator.

Knowledge is power.

Francis Bacon

A really good teacher can teach
and teach and never run out of
things to teach.

Jim Dale

Learning requires hard work and perseverance. The fun, or joy, comes from having learned how to do something and then being able to do it again independently.

Elizabeth Crosby Stull

Small boy to father: "There's a special PTA meeting tonight; just you, my teacher, and the principal."

The Amplifier, Mansfield, Ohio

The first time a student realizes that a little learning is a dangerous thing is when he brings home a poor report card.

Mark Twain

All good students recognize when it happens: the blessing of being taught by a teacher whose thinking is so elegant, whose method is so impeccable, that we can only sit back in mute wonder and gratitude at being allowed to witness the intricate workings of a superior mind.

Lorraine Glennon and Mary Mohler

Education is not the filling of a pail,
but the lighting of a fire.

William Butler Yeats

A child must learn early to believe
that she is somebody worthwhile,
and that she can do many
praiseworthy things.

Benjamin Mays

T aking her kindergarten class to the petting zoo, Mrs. Ganio gave each child a turn identifying animals. Finally it was young Bess's turn. Pointing to a deer, the teacher asked, "Now what is the name of that animal?" Bess looked long and hard, but was unable to come up with the answer. "Think," the teacher encouraged. "What does your mommy call your daddy at home?" Suddenly the girl's face brightened. "So that's what a horse's ass looks like?"

Jeff Rovin

To the thousands of good teachers across our nation, hats off to you. Yours is a high calling. Please don't stop. Never give up. If ever we needed you, we need you now.

Mark W. Merrill

TEACHER: "Where are the Andes, Debby?"
DEBBY: "At the end of the armies, Ma'am."

Rosy Border

Mankind owes to the child the best it has to give.

United Nations declaration

A teacher has two jobs: fill young minds with knowledge, yes, but more important, give those minds a compass so that that knowledge doesn't go to waste.

Principal Jacobs in *Mr. Holland's Opus*

Only the educated are free.

Epictetus

Teachers teach because they care.
Teaching young people is what they
do best.

Horace Mann

Even though the moral and character development of our students is primarily the responsibility of their parents and the community, teachers are expected to set a standard of high morals and good character.

Patricia Woodward

TEACHER: "If I had fifty apples in my right hand and thirty apples in my left hand, what would I have?"
DEBBY: "Big hands."

Rosy Border

There's many a best seller that could have been prevented by a good teacher.

Flannery O'Connor

A little girl arrived at kindergarten all out of breath with excitement.

"Why, what's the matter?" asked her teacher.

"We've got a new baby at our house," she replied. "Won't you come and see it?"

"Oh, thanks!" said the teacher. "But I think I had better wait until your mother is better."

"It's all right," said the girl. "You don't have to be afraid—it's not catching."

Lewis and Faye Copeland

Children are our most valuable
natural resource.

Herbert Hoover

I was taught that it is not enough just
to live my life. I was placed on this
planet to make a difference in the
lives of others.

Edward J. Silver Jr.

There are more students in our schools today than ever before, and we're asking you to teach every one of them to high standards. That's a tall order. Yet you've moved us forward, and I'm proud of each and every one of you.

Richard W. Riley

Sign in a Vassar math class: Girls, watch your figures.

Helen Rudin

Great teachers empathize with kids, respect them, and believe that each one has something special that can be built upon.

Ann Lieberman

You can learn many things from children. How much patience you have, for instance.

Franklin P. Jones

Q: Why is the school basketball court always so soggy?
A: Because the players are always dribbling.

Rosy Border

Learning is always rebellion
. . . every bit of new truth is
revolutionary to what was
believed before.

Margaret Lee Runbeck

We're here to help children succeed.
It's that simple.

Elaine Collins

The best teacher is one who never forgets what it is like to be a student. The best administrator is one who never forgets what it is like to be a teacher.

Neila A. Connors

Too often we give children answers to remember rather than problems to solve.

Roger Lewin

Great teachers are terminally curious and have a penchant for lifelong learning.

Jimmy Fay and David Funk

For some reason, everyone but Lenore got the wrong answer on the science test.

"Tell me," the teacher asked her after returning the papers, "how did you know that heat causes objects to expand, and cold causes them to shrink?"

"Because I'm no dope," she said. "In the summer, when it's hot, the days are longer. And in the winter, when it's cold, they're shorter."

Jeff Rovin

We shouldn't teach great books; we should teach a love of reading.

B. F. Skinner

HARRY: "I don't think my woodshop teacher likes me much."
GARY: "What makes you think that?"
HARRY: "He's teaching me to make a coffin!"

Rosy Border

The gains in education are never really lost. Books may be burned and cities sacked, but truth, like the yearning for freedom, lives in the hearts of humble men.

Franklin D. Roosevelt

The more we study the more we discover our ignorance.

Percy Bysshe Shelley

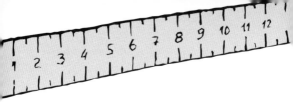

Everyone who remembers his own educational experience remembers teachers, not methods and techniques.

Sydney Hook

Teacher's True Story

Trying to get Kyle to eat healthy, I said, "Eat your peas. It will make your eyes sparkle." Joey overheard me and blurted out, "Teacher—my cat's eyes sparkle!"

I replied, "That's nice. Does your cat eat peas?"

"No," responded Joey, "but he drinks water out of the toilet."

Martha Gillham

Nothing you do for a child
is ever wasted.

Garrison Keillor

Education: a debt due from present
to future generations.

George Peabody

Bear in mind that the wonderful things you learn in your schools are the work of many generations. All this is put in your hands as your inheritance in order that you may receive it, honor it, add to it, and one day faithfully hand it on to your children.

Albert Einstein

If you are a wise man you will observe your pupil carefully before saying a word to him.

Jean Jacques Rousseau

TEACHER: "Which is farther away, England or the moon?"
JOHNNY: "England."
TEACHER: "England? What makes you think that?"
JOHNNY: "'Cause we can see the moon and we can't see England."

Lewis and Faye Copeland

Children are living messages we send to a world we will not see.

Amish proverb

One morning as I was teaching a second-grade class, Andy arrived at school in an excited mood. His family had just acquired a new dog, and he was bubbling over in his description of their new pet. "What color is your dog?" I asked. Without hesitation he answered, "Pitch white!"

Teaching is a daily exercise
in vulnerability.

Parker Palmer

When I was in school, I cheated on
my metaphysics exam: I looked into
the soul of the boy sitting next to me.

Woody Allen

People who aren't in education just don't know what they're missing.

Keith Blue

It's the less bright students who make teachers teach better.

Malcolm Forbes

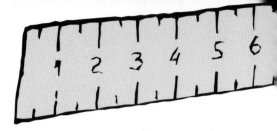

Knowing that we're valued and being in the presence of people who want to share with us something of this world that they love are the two most important ingredients in education.

Fred Rogers

A substitute teacher in a downtown public school surveyed her class the first morning she was assigned a job and sent a hurry call for the principal. "Help!" she demanded. "They're all here!"

Bennett Cerf

Get over the idea that only children should spend their time in study. Be a student so long as you still have something to learn, and this will mean all your life.

Henry Doherty

Let us put our minds together and see what kind of life we can make for our children.

Sitting Bull

We are most nearly ourselves when we achieve the seriousness of the child at play.

Heraclitus

TEACHER: "Spell 'straight.'"
PUPIL: "S-T-R-A-I-G-H-T."
TEACHER: "Correct. What does it mean?"
PUPIL: "Without ginger ale."

Lewis and Faye Copeland

When you reach the end of your rope, tie a knot in it and hang on.

Thomas Jefferson